A Gloucester Press Library Edition

Imperial Rome

CONTENTS

© Aladdin Books Ltd

Designed and produced by
Aladdin Books Ltd
70 Old Compton Street
London W1

First published in the
United States in 1985 by
Gloucester Press
387 Park Avenue South
New York NY 10016

ISBN 0-531-17003-9

Library of Congress
Catalog Card No. 85-80644

*Certain illustrations have previously appeared in the ''Civilization Library''
series published by Gloucester Press.*

THE CIVILIZATION LIBRARY

Imperial Rome

JILL HUGHES

Illustrated by
IVAN LAPPER

Consultant
P. D. POWELL

Gloucester Press
New York · Toronto · 1985

Village to empire

The city of Rome began in the eighth century BC, as a small village of huts on the Palatine – one of the seven hills of Rome. As the city grew it attracted the attention of its powerful neighbor, the Etruscan kingdom to the north.

Etruscan kings ruled Rome until 509 BC when the Romans drove out the proud King Tarquin. By this time the people hated kings and so the city became a "republic," ruled by a council called the "senate."

Rome soon conquered all the other Italian peoples, including the Etruscans. By 146 BC Rome had even captured the great North African city of Carthage, together with its colonies which were dotted around the Mediterranean.

Rome, 300 AD: magnificent marble temples rise above a collection of markets established by various emperors.

The end of the republic

The Roman army was now a powerful fighting force, and made conquests in Greece and the east. As Rome gained more territories, the profits of war flowed back in the form of treasure and tribute. Thousands of captives were seized and put to work as slaves.

But the powerful army generals began to quarrel with each other and the senate, leading to bitter civil wars. Julius Caesar emerged victorious from these, but he was assassinated in 44 BC. His nephew Octavian became ruler. Later, renamed Augustus, he became the first emperor of the Roman world.

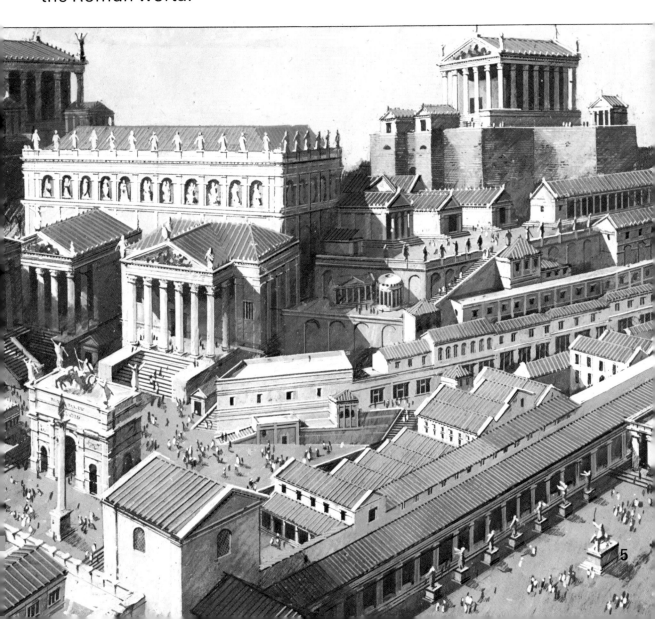

An emperor attended by the praetorian guard.

Power politics

As head of state Augustus had been voted the power that had once belonged to elected republican leaders. It was this power which made him, and his successors, "emperors." Emperors were not kings, so their sons did not automatically succeed them. Instead, they named the men they wanted to follow them: sometimes they were relatives, sometimes colleagues. In practice the next emperor was often chosen by the powerful "praetorian guard," a bodyguard originally set up by Augustus.

Emperors made outside Rome

The first few emperors after Augustus were all descendants of Julius Caesar. Some were good, like Claudius (41-54 AD), but Nero (54-68 AD) was cruel and extravagant. He committed suicide and for a year rival candidates struggled to become emperor. Vespasian, a good soldier, eventually won with the support of the army in the east and on the River Danube. He was the first emperor "made outside Rome."

Portrait busts of three important emperors

Augustus
ruled 27 BC-14 AD

Trajan, a Spaniard,
ruled 98-117 AD

Hadrian, a Spaniard,
ruled 117-138 AD

Politics and religion

The senate had existed since earliest times; even after Rome became an empire, with an emperor, it continued to function. The members of the senate were divided into two classes, and they elected officers, or "consuls," who administered all parts of the empire and the army.

The gods

All Romans had a great respect for religion and most homes had shrines to the household gods, or "lares," who were thought of as the protectors of the hearth and home.

After his death, Augustus was declared a god, as were most emperors, which shows that the people had great reverence for the government. The Romans were allowed to worship foreign gods – such as the Egyptian Isis and the Persian Mithras – so long as they remained loyal to the Roman state. The Pantheon (right) was built by the Emperor Hadrian as a temple to many of Rome's gods.

The senators' meeting house was called the "curia." They met there to discuss laws and advise on policy.

The Roman army

When the Romans first conquered Italy they did so with a citizen army of volunteers, but by the time of the republican civil wars there was a permanent, "professional" army, which was needed to keep peace throughout the empire. Roman citizens fought in the legions, but other peoples were recruited as auxiliaries – they often had special skills like the Syrian archers or Spanish cavalrymen.

After twenty years' service a legionary got a pension and some land. An auxiliary was given Roman citizenship.

A legion consisted of about 5,500 men. Each legion had its own standard, crowned with a silver imperial eagle. To lose a standard was a terrible disgrace. There were ten units, called cohorts, in a legion, and six centuries (of 80 to 100 men) in each cohort. Centuries were commanded by centurions, who formed the backbone of the army.

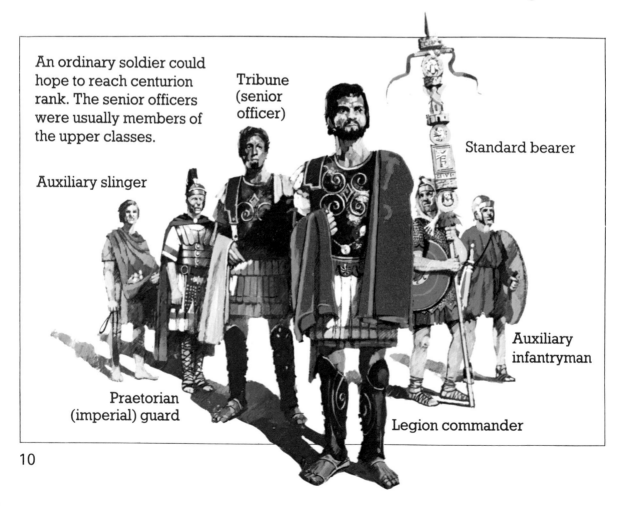

An ordinary soldier could hope to reach centurion rank. The senior officers were usually members of the upper classes.

Auxiliary slinger

Tribune (senior officer)

Standard bearer

Auxiliary infantryman

Praetorian (imperial) guard

Legion commander

Here the Romans are attacking a city in Dacia (modern Rumania) during Trajan's campaign. The legionaries are using a siege tower. Once hauled against the walls, a platform drops down, and the soldiers surge across to engage the enemy on the ramparts.

On the ground below, the soldiers often group together to raise their shields above their heads to form a protective "tortoise."

11

Life on the frontier

Some parts of the empire were always troublesome, like the Rhine frontier, where the German tribes were never really subdued. Legions could be moved to trouble spots if necessary. Augustus reorganized the army into 28 legions, and for the next two hundred years no more than 30 were needed to hold the frontiers. When the army marched out to battle, the commander and his escort were followed by the cavalry, the catapults and siege machines, the officers and the standard bearers and then the main body of foot soldiers or "infantry."

Cavalry units were usually drawn from provinces with a tradition of horsemanship. The Batavians (from the area now called Holland) were famous horsemen.

Forts and towns

On the march the army set up temporary camps. When territory was conquered more permanent forts were built and eventually the civilian population was encouraged to build towns on the Roman pattern. Soldiers would farm plots of land around their forts, and towns were also established for veteran soldiers. Forts and towns all over the empire repeated the same rectangular grid pattern as the Roman marching camp, with straight streets crossing at right angles.

A military settlement

The final frontier

The map shows the size of the Roman world when Hadrian became emperor in 117 AD. The main boundaries had been fixed since the time of Augustus along natural frontiers like the Rhine and the Danube in Europe, and the deserts of Africa and the Middle East. New provinces were added by military campaigns like Trajan's against Dacia (modern Rumania) in 101-105 AD.

Governing the provinces

Conquered territories were made into provinces ruled by governors, and tax collectors gathered revenue for Rome. Legions of the army were stationed where rebellions might break out, and Roman law was enforced throughout the empire. Latin was spoken in the west, Greek in the east.

Atlantic Ocean

York

London

Paris

Bordeaux

Marseilles

Cordoba

Cadiz

Tangier

The Roman world when the Emperor Hadrian came to power in 117 AD. A huge wall was built by his forces between England and Scotland, marking the northern limit of Roman imperial power.

Key to map

Boundary of Roman Empire

Scale in miles

0   250   500

Caspian Sea

Black Sea

Milan

Sarmizegetusa

Split

Rome
Ostia
Pompeii

Constantinople

Athens

Tarsus

Dura-Europus

Rhodes

Palmyra

Carthage

Mediterranean Sea

Jerusalem

Leptis Magna

Alexandria

From left to right are some of the people ruled by Rome: a helmeted Parthian; a German with a topknot; an Egyptian; a painted Pict; a Scotsman; two Germans with shields; an Asian tribesman; a Greek; a Phrygian in a cap; and Jews from the province of Judaea.

15

Supplying the City

Augustus had added the province of Egypt to the empire, and grain from the fertile Nile valley supplemented the huge shipments already supplied by Africa. Six million sacks of grain a year were shipped in to Ostia, the port of Rome.

Produce from the empire

Merchants and traders followed, or in some cases, went before the legions. There were even Roman traders on the coast of India. Goods of all sorts flowed into Rome – silks and spices came from the east; glass from Syria; papyrus (which was made into paper) from Egypt; pottery and cloth from Gaul; tin, copper and lead from Spain.

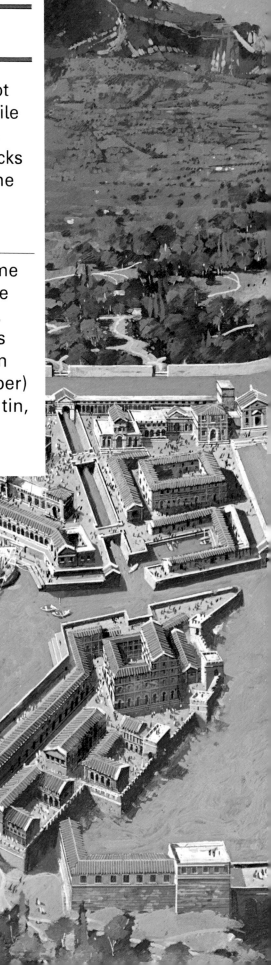

Sea lanes

The empire was large and communications were slow, but if the weather was fine, journey times could be reduced by sea. The writer Pliny tells us Africa could be reached from Ostia in two days, Spain in four. A ship's capacity was measured in "amphorae," large pottery jars in which cargoes were packed for transport.

Unloading and storage

When the sturdy merchant ships unloaded at Ostia, their cargoes were stored in big warehouses called "horrea." Trajan built more of these as well as large granaries. Barges pulled by oxen carried goods on the last leg of the journey to Rome itself.

A reconstruction of the port of Ostia. It has a lighthouse at its entrance to guide ships inside. The inner harbor is fringed with granaries and warehouses.

17

Engineering

The Romans were the greatest road builders the world has ever seen. Roman military surveyors developed ways of measuring, planning and putting up huge bridges and aqueducts using new materials like concrete (a quick-setting mixture of rubble and cement) and structures like the arch (which can carry a great weight over a wide span). Roman soldiers carried road-building materials with them, and the straight Roman roads marked their passage across the empire.

A good water supply

Roman cities needed water for drinking, for public baths and even for heating buildings! Two huge aqueducts transported fresh water from the hills around Rome in lead pipes. The pipes were carried across the valleys on the great arches of the Aqua Claudia and the Aqua Marcia aqueducts. One branch of the Carthage aqueduct was 132km (82 miles) long.

Gangs of slaves were employed on many state building projects. The Romans used cranes and pulleys invented by the Greeks, but pioneered the use of cement and concrete.

One of the most spectacular aqueducts is at Leptis Magna in North Africa, a town founded for retired Roman soldiers. But not all civil engineering projects were so successful. At Saldae, also in North Africa, military experts were called in when two teams, who were building a tunnel through a mountain, failed to meet in the middle!

Wealth and manufacture

While the Romans were great builders and engineers they never applied technology to manufacturing on a large scale. They had so much wealth from their empire, and so many slaves to work for them, that they had no real need to invent money-saving or labor-saving devices. In fact, many of their machines were quite primitive.

Coins and mints

The earliest Roman coin was a clumsy piece of copper, but something more convenient was needed as the empire expanded and trade grew. Mines in conquered territories provided metals for coinage, and mints were set up all over the empire. Coins bearing the emperor's head were used to pay the army, to pay taxes and to buy and sell goods.

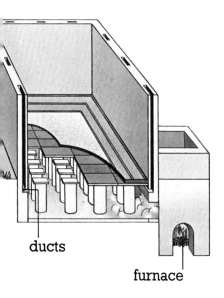

ducts

furnace

The hypocaust system of heating used hot air from a furnace to heat the rooms. The hot air was drawn up through ducts in the floor and walls.

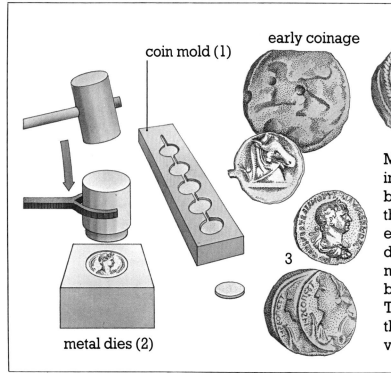

coin mold (1)

early coinage

metal dies (2)

3

4

Molten metal was poured into a mold to make coin blanks (1). The blanks were then struck between "dies" engraved with the coin design (2). Sometimes mistakes were made, and the blank was struck twice! (3) The design on the back of the coin often celebrated a victory, or a new province (4).

Home comforts

With the increase in trade the standard of living for wealthy Romans went up. Their houses had running water, underfloor heating, painted walls, and beautiful mosaic floors. Many of the craftsmen who made mosaics were Greek and had large workshops where they mass-produced mosaic panels and borders.

Applied technology

There were large "factories" in Gaul making textiles and pottery – mainly for army use – but their methods of production were very simple. Spinning was still done by hand without even a spinning wheel. But one area where technology was more successfully applied was in agriculture.

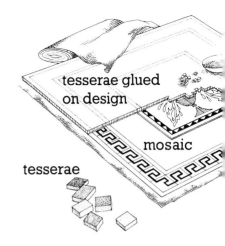

Mosaics were made of small stones called *tesserae*. They could be made in advance by drawing the design on cloth, and glueing the tesserae face down. The whole thing was turned over, dropped in place and the glued-on backing removed with hot water.

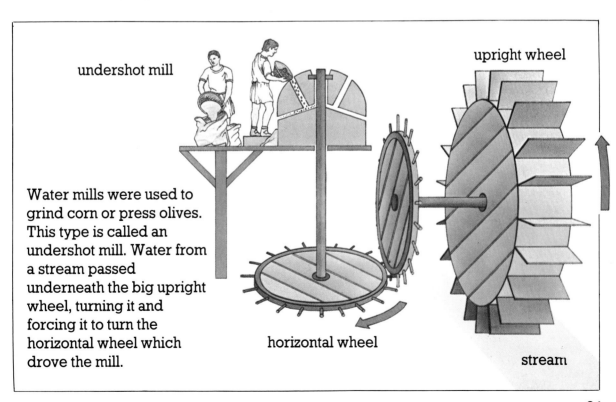

Water mills were used to grind corn or press olives. This type is called an undershot mill. Water from a stream passed underneath the big upright wheel, turning it and forcing it to turn the horizontal wheel which drove the mill.

City life

At the height of the empire Rome was a city of a million people and the place where everyone wanted to be. The writer Juvenal complained of life in Rome with its squalor and overcrowding, where the "rich look after one another and nobody looks after the poor," but he could not tear himself away.

Although the city was full of grand public buildings, accommodation for the ordinary citizen was poor. Many people lived in tenements; these rarely had cooking facilities, so food was bought from cheap food shops and snack bars. There were open shops on the ground floor with rooms for rent above. Fire was a constant hazard, and the tenants on the upper floors threw their garbage out of the windows onto the street below.

A constant bustle

The narrow streets of the city were thronged with people buying and selling, and drinking in the wine shops. The writer Seneca, tutor to the emperor Nero, complained that the noise from the local baths continually disturbed him in his lodgings. All day, wooden-wheeled carts rumbled over the cobbles of the narrow alleys of the city.

Trades of all descriptions were carried on in Rome. Greek slave schoolteachers lived above butchers, who traded next to cobblers or blacksmiths. There were snack bars and wine shops on every corner.

A life of luxury

The rich in Rome lived a life of ease. Men might devote some time to going to the senate, or they might visit their estates to make sure that their slave managers were running things properly. Many Roman patricians rented out slum property in the city, but again they had slaves to supervise their tenements. Unless a man was determined to pursue a political or military career, perhaps with long absences abroad, he filled his days in Rome with pleasure. The most important of these was eating or, rather, dining in style. Rare and exotic foods were sought after – for example, boiled ostrich and nightingales' tongues. The guests lay on couches, where they were served by slaves and entertained by musicians.

Only the very rich could expect to eat huge meals with many courses, flavored with spices and washed down with fine wines. The rich banquets that they enjoyed were produced in cramped kitchens by hard-working slaves. The poor ate little meat and survived on wheat bread and porridge.

A Roman kitchen

During banquets guests often dropped scraps on the floor for the slaves to sweep up. This mosaic is a joke and was called "the unswept floor."

Cruel sports

Rich and poor alike attended the bloodthirsty games in the amphitheater. Here armed gladiators fought each other or animals, to the uproarious approval of the crowd. Wild beasts were imported from all over the empire to thrill the spectators. Condemned criminals, including Christians, were thrown to the lions or forced to fight to the death as part of the brutal spectacle.

A day at the baths

Besides the thrills of the games, Romans could also enjoy chariot racing in the circus. There were four teams, named after colors, and they were as keenly supported as football teams are today. But a quieter form of entertainment was to spend a day at the public baths. Men, women and children could use hot and cold rooms, swimming pools and exercise yards. Bathing was a social activity, and every small town had public baths.

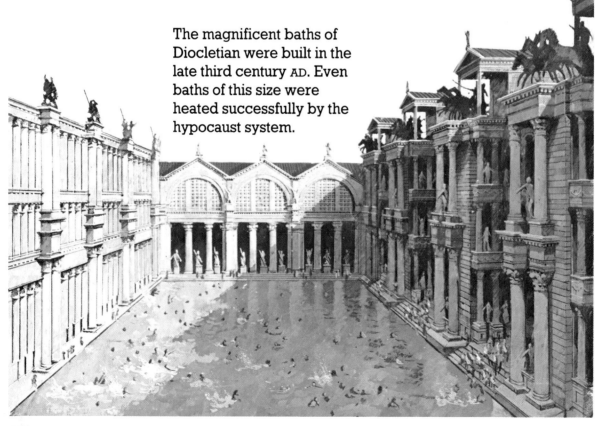

The magnificent baths of Diocletian were built in the late third century AD. Even baths of this size were heated successfully by the hypocaust system.

The Colosseum opened in 80 AD. One of the most popular entertainments was a contest between armed men, and others who just had nets and forks.

The Roman villa

The villa, or country house, could vary in size from a modest farmhouse to a palatial building with separate gardens and a huge estate. On the coast between Rome and Naples, many rich Romans had beautifully decorated sea villas with magnificent sea views. Some had villas in different parts of the country which they could use like "hotels" when they were traveling. But above all, villas were important in the Roman economy as agricultural centers which produced the empire's food.

The farming life

There were huge specialist villa estates, manned by gangs of slaves, which produced particular foodstuffs like olives, grain or mutton. However, the traditional villa was the owner's farmhouse, surrounded by outbuildings for slaves and animals, with a farm producing a mixed crop. It appeared all over the Roman world from Britain to Africa and often survived as an oasis of civilization when the empire fell.

Slaves knock olives from the trees and load them into baskets (below). The large round jars in front of the villa were used to store olive oil or wine.

End of empire

The later empire was beset by problems. In the third century AD there was massive inflation and the currency collapsed. Barbarian tribes like the Goths and Vandals constantly attacked the frontiers, and the sheer size of the empire began to overwhelm the administration. A strong soldier-emperor, Diocletian, divided the empire into east and west in 284 AD and ruled with three co-emperors. Rome was sacked twice by the barbarians – in 410 and 455 AD. In 476 AD Odoacer, a Gothic chief, made himself king of Italy. The empire in the west collapsed, but the eastern half of the empire, with its capital, Constantinople – established by Constantine in 330 AD – survived until 1453 AD.

The legacy of Rome

The Roman road network was not surpassed until this century, and Roman law still forms the basis of many modern legal systems. Latin was the language of the church and learning until the Middle Ages, and influenced many modern languages.

Rediscovery and Renaissance

But the Romans also left behind more visible remains of their splendid, if brutal, empire. The huge baths, temples and palaces inspired people to dig in the ruins and see how such marvels had been made. The rediscovery of Roman architecture, the finding of ancient statues and the great curiosity that people felt about such wonders, inspired the Renaissance – and the beginnings of the modern world.

The ruins of Hadrian's villa at Tivoli, outside Rome, are an enduring reminder of the grandeur that was Rome.

Glossary

Amphitheater A large circular or oval open-air theater.

Amphora (plural amphorae) Large pottery jars for storing wine, oil, etc.

Aqueduct A stone or brick channel, raised on arches, to carry water pipes.

Centurion A regular soldier who was the leader of a century (an army unit of 80 to 100 men).

Horrea Warehouses for storing goods.

Hypocaust A system of underfloor heating.

Lares Household gods or guardian spirits.

Legion The main unit of the Roman army; it contained about 5,000 men, all of whom were Roman citizens.

Mosaic A picture – usually part of a floor – made from fragments of stone called "tesserae."

Praetorian guard 4,500 soldiers specially chosen to guard the emperor. They were based in Rome.

Senate Council of Roman citizens responsible for the financial and foreign policy of the state.

Index

PRINTED IN BELGIUM BY

proost
INTERNATIONAL BOOK PRODUCTION